Two Awesome Free

CH00869240

I want to say "Thank You" for buyin
together a few, awesome free gifts for you.

The Essential Kitchen Series Cooking Hacks & Tips Book

&

100 Delicious New Recipes

These gifts are the perfect add-on to this book and I know
you'll love them.

So visit link below to download you free gift now

www.GoodLivingPublishing.com/essential -kitchen

Contents

Chapter 1 - Vegan Lunches

Whether you are new to the idea of vegan eating, or you have been a vegan for a long while now, chances are good that you are looking for some delicious recipes to add to your repertoire. And when it comes to vegan dieting, lunchtime can be one of the most confusing times of the day. What are you supposed to eat if you can't chow down on cheese and lunchmeat every afternoon? How can you eat something quickly at work if you can't microwave some sort of TV dinner meal that is full meats and dairy products? This book is here to help!

When you read through this book, you will realize that there are plenty of healthy, easy, and affordable options out there for vegan lunches. Most of them can even be made ahead of time and stored until you are ready to eat them. Mason jars make excellent storage for vegan lunches. Soups can be easily reheated in these jars, and salads can be kept with the dressing at the bottom of the jar and the toppings stacked above it, so all you have to do is shake the jar before you eat to combine the ingredients. Whatever you choose to make for your vegan lunch, it should be easy and it shouldn't break the bank!

Let's get started on these tasty vegan midday meals!

Benefits of Vegan Diet

You may be someone who cares a great deal about animals and wants to help put an end to animal cruelty. If you are, then this is probably one of the main reasons why you have been drawn to a vegan diet. However, this is not the only reason people become vegans these days, and for some, it is not even on their minds when they make the decision to switch their lifestyle. There are plenty of other benefits to veganism.

To begin with, a vegan diet is simply much healthier than other alternatives. Since vegan diets focus mostly on the consumption of fruits and vegetables, you will naturally be taking in more of the vitamins, nutrients, and antioxidants that are found in these foods. These nutritious foods will help lower your cholesterol, maintain healthy blood sugar levels, and keep your digestive system moving along smoothly.

Vegan dieting is also a great way to help lose weight. Meats, dairy products, and eggs are full of fat and calories, so when you remove them from your diet, you will be automatically consuming less fat than before. Since veggies are also packed with fiber, you'll be moving the fat out of your system much more quickly as well. All in all, you're sure to see weight loss in no time when you switch to a vegan diet.

If you have problems with lactose intolerance, or even if you just have some mild digestive upset when you consume too much dairy, then your body definitely won't miss it when you cut it out. You can get all your calcium and vitamins from vegetable sources, and you do not need milk products in your diet at all. Your stomach will thank you for making the switch!

Last but not least, when you eat a diet consisting of mostly vegetables and fruits, you will naturally feel much more energetic than you did before. These foods are low in fat and high in fiber, so they allow oxygen to move to your muscles much more quickly and keep you feeling focused and full of energy longer than fatty foods do.

Rest assured that switching to a vegan diet is a healthy decision that will benefit you for years to come!

Common Ingredients in Vegan Lunches

Keep your pantry and refrigerator well stocked with these basic items, and you'll be able to easily prepare a lunch for yourself in no time!

- Carrots
- Spinach
- Cabbage
- Stevia sweetener
- Agave nectar
- Lemon juice
- Whole wheat tortilla wraps
- Leafy greens
- Tomatoes
- Vegan mayonnaise
- Sriracha hot sauce
- Tofu
- Garlic
- Vegetable stock

Chapter 2 - Salads

Salads don't have to be boring. As a matter of fact, they're very exciting when you dress them up the right way—and keeping them vegan is ultra-easy!

Thai Inspired Salad

Add some spice to your life with this mildly spicy Thai inspired salad!

Serves: 2

Ingredients

1 cup water
1 avocado
1/4 cup basil
1/4 cup cilantro
1/4 tsp salt
1/8 tsp cayenne pepper
3/4 inch fresh ginger root
1 packet Stevia sweetener
2 cups spinach
1/2 cup cilantro
1/2 cup basil
1 shredded carrot
1/2 cup sliced red cabbage
1/2 sliced red bell pepper
1/2 sliced cucumber

Instructions

Place avocado in blender with water, cilantro, basil, salt, cayenne, ginger, and Stevia; blend on high until smooth.

Place spinach in a large bowl with cilantro, basil, carrot, cabbage, pepper, and cucumber. Toss together.

Add dressing and toss again to coat thoroughly.

Serve.

Vegan Taco Salad

Walnuts provide the "meat"for this meatless salad!

Serves: 2

Ingredients

1/2 diced avocado
1 chopped tomato
2 hearts of romaine, torn
1/3 bunch chopped cilantro
1/2 chopped red onion
1 tbsp cumin
2 cups walnuts
2 tbsp tamari
1/2 tbsp coriander
1 tsp chili powder
1/4 tsp cayenne pepper

Instructions

Place walnuts in a food processor or blender and chop until chunky.

Scrape into a bowl and stir with coriander, cumin, cayenne, and chili powder.

Stir in tamari.

Combine tomatoes with cilantro, onion, and lemon juice.

Place romaine in serving bowls and top with walnut filling.

Top with tomato salsa and avocado slices.

Serve.

Easiest Fruit Salad Ever

The name says it all! This fruit salad is so easy you'll want to munch on it every afternoon!

Serves: 2

Ingredients

Juice of 2 lemons
1 tbsp powdered sugar
1/2 cup fresh mint leaves
2 cups diced cantaloupe
2 cups diced watermelon
2 cups halved strawberries
1 cup blueberries
1 cup raspberries

Instructions

In a blender, blend lemon juice, mint leaves, and powdered sugar together on high until smooth.

Pour over fruit in a large bowl.

Stir to coat well.

Chill for 1 hour.

Serve.

Coleslaw

Vegan coleslaw is easy to make and even easier to eat!

Serves: 2

Ingredients

- 1/2 shredded onion
- 1/2 shredded white cabbage
- 1 thinly sliced red apple
- 1 sliced carrot
- 1 cup water
- 1 cup washed and drained cashews
- 1 lemon, zested and juiced
- 1 tsp agave nectar
- 1/2 tsp salt

Instructions

Chop cashews in a blender until broken well.

Add lemon juice, lemon zest, water, salt, and agave to blender.

Blend on high until smooth.

Toss this cashew "mayonnaise"with onion, cabbage, and carrot in a large bowl.

Serve topped with apple slices.

Kale Salad

This salad works great on its own or tastes awesome over a bowl of cooked quinoa!

Serves: 2

Ingredients

- 2 diced avocados
- 1 bunch chopped curly kale
- 1 cup soaked sunflower seeds
- 3 tbsp olive oil
- 3 tbsp lemon juice
- 1/2 tsp salt
- 2 crushed cloves of garlic
- 1 tsp black pepper

Instructions

Place chopped kale in a large bowl.

In a separate small bowl, whisk together lemon juice, olive oil, garlic, salt, and pepper.

Pour dressing over kale.

Massage dressing into kale with your hands until kale is very soft.

Toss in diced avocado and sunflower seeds.

Serve.

Tahini Tomato Salad

With a base of kale, this salad is packed with superfoods!

Serves: 2

Ingredients

> 1/4 cup olive oil
> 1/2 cup tahini
> 1/4 cup water
> 2 tbsp lemon juice
> 1 tsp agave nectar
> 1 chipotle chile pepper in adobo sauce, seeded and drained
> 1 tsp ground coriander
> 1 tsp ground cumin
> 1 tsp salt
> 1 diced tomato
> 1 chopped bunch of kale
> 4 tsp hemp seeds

Instructions

In a blender, combine oil, tahini, lemon juice, agave, chipotle, coriander, cumin, and salt; blend on high until smooth.

Toss kale in a large bowl with tahini dressing.

Massage the kale with your hands until very soft and coated with dressing.

Serve topped with tomato and hemp seeds.

Cucumber Salad

Light and oh so tasty, this salad is the perfect meal to cool you down on a hot summer's day.

Serves: 2

Ingredients

> 2 tbsp olive oil
> 3 tbsp white wine vinegar
> 1 tsp Stevia sweetener
> 10oz halved grape tomatoes
> 3 thinly sliced cucumbers
> 2 tbsp chopped dill
> 1/2 thinly sliced Vidalia onion
> 1/4 tsp black pepper
> 1/4 tsp salt

Instructions

Whisk olive oil with vinegar and Stevia in a small bowl.

In a large bowl, toss together cucumbers, onion, tomatoes, dill, salt, and pepper.

Pour over dressing and toss to coat well.

Let stand at room temperature for 20 minutes.

Serve.

Broccoli Salad

This salad incorporates the creamiest dressing you will ever taste—without any actual cream in it!

Serves: 2

Ingredients

1 cup sunflower seeds
6 cups bite-sized pieces of broccoli
1/2 cup raisins
1/2 cup chopped red onion
1/3 cup water
1 cup raw soaked cashews
1 tbsp lemon juice
1-1/2 tbsp apple cider vinegar
1 tbsp chopped shallot
1 tbsp maple syrup
1/2 tsp salt
1 chopped clove of garlic
1/2 tsp Dijon mustard

Instructions

Place cashews in a blender and blend on high until chopped well.

Add water, vinegar, lemon juice, maple syrup, garlic, salt, and mustard; blend on high until smooth.

Stir in shallot.

Toss broccoli, red onion, raisins, and sunflower seeds in a large bowl with dressing until coated evenly.

Serve.

Blood Orange Salad

The winter colors in this salad are incredible!

Serves: 2

Ingredients

1 tbsp orange juice
1 tbsp olive oil
1 tbsp cider vinegar
1 tsp dried thyme
2 tsp agave nectar
1 julienned carrot
4 cups baby lettuce
2 sliced blood oranges
1 julienned red beet
3/4 cup soaked and dried almonds

Instructions

Whisk together juice, oil, vinegar, thyme, and agave in a small bowl.

In a separate bowl, combine lettuce with beets, carrots, and oranges.

Pour over dressing and toss to coat well.

Serve topped with almonds.

Fennel Salad

This is a fancy salad that can be plated beautifully for a formal occasion, or you can casually munch on it anytime!

Serves: 2

Ingredients

1/4 cup and 1 tbsp olive oil
Juice of 1/2 lemon
2 tbsp maple syrup
1 tbsp diced shallot
1 cup soaked and rinsed macadamia nuts
1 tsp nutritional yeast
1 tbsp agave syrup
2 tbsp diced fennel leaves
1/4 tsp salt
1/4 tsp black pepper
1 thinly sliced apple
1/2 cup whole walnuts
2 thinly sliced fennel bulbs

Instructions

Blend together 1/4 cup olive oil with maple syrup and lemon juice in a blender on high until smooth.

Stir in shallots and set aside mixture.

In the blender, process 1 tbsp olive oil with macadamia nuts, agave, yeast, fennel leaves, salt, and pepper.

Toss apple and fennel slices in previously-made vinaigrette.

Plate with alternating apple and fennel slices.

Top with macadamia mixture, walnuts, and extra black pepper if desired.

Serve.

Chapter 3 - Soups

Vegan soups are easy to make and even easier to enjoy. When you want something warm for lunch, grab a soup—you can even make them ahead of time and keep them in mason jars for easy reheating and eating!

Creamy Cauliflower Soup

There are no potatoes and no cream in this soup at all—the creaminess all comes from the healthy cauliflower!

Serves: 3

Ingredients

1/4 cup olive oil
2 heads cauliflower florets
1 chopped onion
6 cups water
4 cloves chopped garlic
Salt and pepper to taste

Instructions

Soak cauliflower for 20 minutes in lightly salted water, then drain and place on a baking sheet.

Preheat oven broiler.

Broil cauliflower in oven for 30 minutes to brown.

In a large pot on the stove over medium heat, cook onion for 5 minutes.

Stir in garlic and roasted cauliflower, then add salt, pepper, and water.

Simmer for 30 minutes uncovered.

Blend with an immersion blender or place in a blender and puree on high until smooth.

Serve.

Hot and Sour Soup

Get your Asian soup fix with this easy recipe!

Serves: 4

Ingredients

4 dried shiitake mushrooms
1oz dried wood ear mushrooms
2 cups hot water
12 dried tiger lily buds
1/3oz bamboo fungus
5 tbsp rice vinegar
3 tbsp soy sauce
1/4 cup cornstarch
8oz container of firm tofu, cut into strips
1/4 tsp crushed red pepper flakes
1 quart vegetable broth
1/2 tsp black pepper
1/2 tbsp sesame oil
1/2 tbsp chili oil
1 sliced green onion

Instructions

Soak mushrooms and lily buds for 20 minutes in hot water, then drain and save liquid.

Slice mushrooms and cut lily buds in half.

Soak bamboo fungus in hot water for 20 minutes, then drain and mince.

In a small bowl, blend vinegar, soy sauce, and 1 tbsp cornstarch, then place 1/2 of the tofu strips in the mixture.

In a pot on the stove over medium-high heat, combine reserved mushroom liquid with vegetable broth and bring to a boil.

Stir in mushrooms and lily buds, then turn heat to low and simmer for 5 minutes.

Stir in red pepper and black pepper.

In a small bowl, combine remaining corn starch and remaining water, then stir into soup to thicken.

In the pot, combine remaining tofu strips with soy sauce mixture.

Bring back to a boil, then stir in chili oil, sesame oil, and bamboo fungus.

Serve with green onion.

Lentil Soup

Exotic flavor abounds in this tasty and healthful lentil soup.

Serves: 4

Ingredients

1 chopped onion
1 tbsp peanut oil
1 tbsp minced fresh ginger root
1 pinch fenugreek seeds
1 chopped clove of garlic
1 cup dry red lentils
1/3 cup chopped fresh cilantro
1 cup peeled, seeded, and cubed butternut squash
14oz canned coconut milk
2 cups water
1 tsp curry powder
2 tbsp tomato paste
1 pinch ground nutmeg
1 pinch cayenne pepper
1/4 tsp salt
1/4 tsp black pepper

Instructions

In a pot over medium heat, cook onion, garlic, ginger, and fenugreek in oil for 5 minutes.

Stir in squash, lentils, and cilantro and cook for 1 moreminute.

Stir in coconut milk, water, tomato paste, curry powder, nutmeg, cayenne, pepper, and salt.

Bring to a boil, then reduce heat to low and simmer uncovered for 30 minutes.

Serve.

Borscht

This traditional soup can be easily made vegan style with just a few simple tweaks!

Serves: 4

Ingredients

3 minced cloves of garlic
4 tbsp olive oil
1 chopped onion
2 chopped stalks of celery
2 chopped carrots
3 diced beets, including greens
1 chopped green bell pepper
16oz canned whole peeled tomatoes
2 quartered potatoes
1/2 cup canned peeled and diced tomatoes
2 cups vegetable broth
1 cup shredded Swiss chard
4 cups water
2 tbsp dried dill weed
1/4 tsp black pepper
1/4 tsp salt
16oz package silken tofu

Instructions

In a skillet over medium heat, cook garlic and onion in 1 tbsp oil for 5 minutes.

Heat remaining oil in a large pot over medium-high heat, then cook carrots, celery, beets, bell pepper, whole and diced tomatoes, chard, potatoes, and onion mixture; stir and cook for 8 minutes.

Stir in water, broth, dill, pepper, and salt, and bring to a boil.

Reduce heat to low and simmer for 1 hour.

Strain half of the beets from the soup mixture and blend on high until smooth.

Add tofu and puree again until smooth.

Stir mixture back into pot.

Simmer until mixture is reduced by 1/3—approximately 1 morehour.

Serve warm or chill for 2 hours before serving.

Minestrone

Pack some super foods into your diet with this ultra-healthy soup! Serve it alongside some garlic wheat bread for a perfect lunch.

Serves: 4

Ingredients

1 chopped onion
1 tbsp vegetable oil
2 chopped stalks of celery
2-1/2 tsp Italian seasoning
1/4 tsp black pepper
1/4 tsp salt
5 cups vegetable broth
28oz canned Italian-style diced tomatoes
2 sliced carrots
2 diced sweet potatoes
6oz chopped green beans
5 minced cloves of garlic

Instructions

In a pot on the stove over medium-high heat, cook onion, celery, salt, pepper, and Italian seasoning in oil for 5 minutes.

Stir in tomatoes and juice from can, sweet potatoes, broth, green beans, carrots, and garlic.

Bring to a boil, then reduce heat to low and simmer for 30 minutes, stirring occasionally.

Serve.

Corn Chowder

A warm corn chowder on a cold winter's night is a perfect, homey comfort food.

Serves: 4

Ingredients

1 chopped onion
2 tbsp olive oil
1 cup chopped carrots
1 cup chopped celery
1 minced clove of garlic
2 cubes vegetable bouillon
2-1/2 cups water
2 cups soy milk
2 cups corn
1 tbsp flour
1 tsp garlic powder
1 tsp dried parsley
1 tsp black pepper
1 tsp salt

Instructions

In a large skillet over medium heat, cook onions and celery in oil for 7 minutes.

Stir in carrots and garlic and cook for 5 moreminutes.

Boil water in a pot over high heat, then stir in bouillon and reduce heat to medium.

After bouillon has dissolved completely, add corn and skillet vegetables.

Simmer until vegetables are tender, then turn heat to low and stir in soy milk.

Quickly whisk in flour to thicken.

Stir in garlic powder, parsley, pepper, and salt.

Cook while stirring constantly for 15 minutes to thicken.

Serve.

Beany Soup

You'll get plenty of fiber from this soup; it's packed with healthy beans!

Serves: 4

Ingredients

1 chopped onion
1 tbsp olive oil
1 chopped rib of celery
1 tsp thyme
1 tbsp crushed garlic
8 cups vegetable broth
15oz canned black beans, drained
15oz canned white beans, drained
1 tsp ground cumin
1/2 tsp dried sage

Instructions

In a large pot on the stove over medium heat, cook onion, garlic, celery, and thyme in oil for 10 minutes.

Add vegetable broth, black beans, and cumin, and cook for 1 minute.

Add white beans and sage and bring to a gentle boil.

Simmer for 30 minutes.

Serve.

Peanut Soup

This recipe combines African flavors for a unique taste experience you'll want to enjoy again and again!

Serves: 5

Ingredients

    2 chopped onions
    2 tbsp olive oil
    2 chopped red bell peppers
    4 minced cloves of garlic
    8 cups vegetable broth
    28oz canned crushed tomatoes in liquid
    1/4 tsp black pepper
    1/4 tsp chili powder
    1/2 cup uncooked brown rice
    2/3 cup extra crunchy peanut butter

Instructions

In a large pot on the stove over medium-high heat, cook onions and bell peppers in oil for 5 minutes.

Add garlic and cook for 1 minute more.

Stir in vegetable stock, tomatoes, chili powder, and pepper.

Turn heat to low and simmer uncovered for 30 minutes.

Stir in rice, cover, and let simmer 15 minutes more.

Stir in peanut butter until blended.

Serve.

Carrot Soup

Serve up this easy soup that only has five ingredients for a quick and spicy lunch!

Serves: 4

Ingredients

1 chopped onion
2 tbsp vegetable oil
1 tbsp curry powder
4 cups vegetable broth
2 chopped pounds of carrots

Instructions

In a large pot on the stove over medium heat, cook onion in oil for 5 minutes.

Stir in curry powder and cook 1 minute more.

Add carrots and stir to coat.

Pour in broth and simmer, uncovered, for 20 minutes. Do not boil.

Place mixture into a blender and blend on high until smooth.

Pour back into pot and thin with water if soup is too thick.

Serve.

Gazpacho

Soup isn't just for cold days! Make this chilled vegan style soup for a hot summer afternoon.

Serves: 5

Ingredients

1 minced onion
4 cups tomato juice
1 chopped cucumber
1 minced green bell pepper
2 chopped green onions
2 cups chopped tomatoes
1 minced clove of garlic
2 tbsp red wine vinegar
3 tbsp lemon juice
1 tsp dried basil
1 tsp dried tarragon
1 tsp Stevia sweetener
1/4 cup chopped fresh parsley
1/4 tsp salt
1/4 tsp black pepper

Instructions

Place tomato juice in a blender with bell pepper, onion, tomatoes, cucumber, garlic, green onions, lemon juice, tarragon, vinegar, parsley, basil, salt, Stevia, and pepper.

Blend on high until still somewhat chunky.

Cover and chill for 2 hours or more before serving.

Serve with a garnish of more parsley.

Chapter 4 - Sandwiches

When soup and salad aren't quite enough for you, give a sandwich a try. If you're looking for something even heartier, pair a half-sandwich with a soup or a salad from the previous chapters!

Barbecue Sandwich

This tempeh-based sandwich is a great energy boost in the middle of the day!

Serves: 2

Ingredients

1/2 block tempeh, cut into 4 pieces
1 sliced sweet potato
1/4 grated onion
1 tsp grapeseed oil
3/4 cup natural ketchup
1 minced clove of garlic
1 tbsp Sriracha hot sauce
2 tbsp apple cider vinegar
2 tbsp maple syrup
1 tbsp Worcestershire sauce
2 toasted crusty rolls, sliced in half
Toppings of your choice (tomato, sprouts, avocado, onion, etc.)

Instructions

In a small pot on the stove over medium heat, cook onion and garlic in oil for 1 minute.

Stir in vinegar, ketchup, maple syrup, Sriracha, and Worcestershire and stir; bring to a gentle boil.

Reduce heat and simmer for 10 minutes to thicken.

In a separate pot, place sweet potatoes and tempeh pieces and cover with about 1 inch of water.

Simmer over low heat for 8 minutes.

Remove to a plate, pat dry, and preheat your oven broiler.

Arrange tempeh and sweet potatoes on a baking sheet and brush with plenty of barbecue sauce.

Broil until slightly charred; flip and baste with barbecue sauce as desired.

Serve on bread with toppings of your choice.

Chard Sandwich

Get tons of healthful chard in your diet when you incorporate this easy sandwich!

Serves: 1

Ingredients

> Baby rainbow Swiss chard, as much as desired
> 2 slices bread
> 2 sliced radishes
> 1 sliced tomato
> Vegan butter, as much as desired
> 2 tbsp white bean spread

Instructions

Spread white bean spread onto each slice of bread.

Layer one slice of bread with chard to taste, and top with tomato slices.

Layer other slice of bread with radishes.

Close sandwich and spread both sides with butter.

Grill in a skillet over medium heat until both sides are golden.

Serve.

Banh Mi

Get back to vegan basics with this tasty tofu-based sandwich!

Serves: 4

Ingredients

2 tbsp soy sauce
1 package extra firm tofu, sliced
1 tbsp rice vinegar
1 tbsp sesame oil
1/4 tsp ground ginger
2 tsp agave nectar
Pinch of red pepper flakes
Pinch of salt
1 large baguette, sliced into four, halved
1 sliced red onion
1 handful cilantro leaves
Sriracha hot sauce, as much as desired

Instructions

Preheat oven to 400 degrees Fahrenheit; line a baking sheet with tin foil.

In a small bowl, combine soy sauce with rice vinegar, sesame oil, agave nectar, ginger, salt, and red pepper flakes.

Dip tofu in sauce and place on baking sheet.

Bake for 15 minutes, then flip and bake 15 minutes more.

Layer tofu on one half of each piece of baguette.

Top with red onion, cilantro, and Sriracha.

Close sandwich and serve.

Faux Egg Salad

No need to eat real eggs; this sandwich tastes even better than the real thing!

Serves: 2

Ingredients

1 tsp yellow mustard seeds
1/3 cup golden raisins
1/4 cup apple cider vinegar
2 tbsp roasted pumpkin seeds
1 pound extra firm tofu
1 chopped scallion
1/2 cup vegan mayonnaise
1 tbsp chopped parsley
3/4 tsp salt
2 tbsp curry powder
1/4 tsp black pepper
4 slices of bread
Toppings of your choice

Instructions

Boil apple cider vinegar, then pour over raisins and mustard seeds and let soak 10 minutes.

Rinse and drain tofu, then crumble it gently in a large bowl.

Add raisins and mustard seeds, scallions, pumpkin seeds, and parsley.

In a separate bowl, combine mayonnaise with salt, pepper, and curry powder.

Stir mixture into tofu until completely combined.

Spread onto bread and top with toppings of your choice.

Serve.

Veggie Wrap

Grill up some delicious vegetables for this exotic twist on a classic lunch!

Serves: 3

Ingredients

    1/2 cup cherry tomatoes
    1 zucchini
    1 red bell pepper
    4 tbsp olive oil
    1 clove garlic
    1 carrot
    1/4 cup vegetable stock
    14oz rinsed and drained chickpeas
    1 tbsp tahini
    2 tsp garam masala
    3 wheat tortilla wraps

Instructions

Preheat oven broiler.

Halve tomatoes and zucchinis; slice pepper and carrot.

Place all veggies on a baking sheet and broil until just charring.

Place chickpeas in blender with carrot, garlic, vegetable stock, olive oil, garam masala, and tahini; blend on high until smooth to make a hummus.

Slice vegetables for easy assembly.

Spread hummus onto each wrap and top with vegetables.

Serve.

Chickpea Salad

This tasty and filling sandwich is perfect for a quick lunch!

Serves: 2

Ingredients

1/2 cup diced carrots
15oz canned drained and rinsed chickpeas
1/2 cup sliced celery
1/4 cup vegan mayonnaise
1/3 cup sliced scallions
1 tbsp lemon juice
Dash of paprika
4 slices thick bread
Leafy greens to taste
1 mashed avocado

Instructions

Mash chickpeas in a large bowl with a fork.

Stir in carrots, celery, mayonnaise, lemon juice, paprika, and scallions until well combined.

Spread onto 2 slices of bread.

Spread other 2 slices with mashed avocado.

Top avocado with leafy greens to taste.

Close sandwiches and serve.

Grilled "Cheese"

Who says you need cheese to make a grilled cheese sandwich?

Serves: 4

Ingredients

- 1-1/2 cups fresh or frozen corn kernels
- 1/2 tsp smoked paprika
- 1/4 cup vegetable broth
- 15oz canned white beans
- 1 tsp cumin
- 1 tsp minced garlic
- 1/2 tsp liquid smoke
- 1/4 tsp salt
- 1/4 tsp black pepper
- 1/4 cup fresh chopped basil
- 5 tbsp water
- 1/2 cup soaked raw cashews
- 1 tsp white miso
- 2 tbsp nutritional yeast
- 1-1/2 tsp ancho chili powder
- 1/2 tsp garlic powder
- 1 baguette
- 2 thinly sliced roma tomatoes
- Vegan mozzarella shreds, to taste

Instructions

Preheat oven to 450 degrees Fahrenheit; line a baking sheet with parchment paper.

Spread corn onto baking sheet and season with salt, pepper, and paprika; toss to coat.

Roast for 10 minutes, then let cool.

Combine 1 cup roasted corn with white beans, vegetable broth, garlic, cumin, liquid smoke, and basil in a blender or food processor.

Blend on high until smooth.

Add remaining corn and pulse a few times until chunky.

Clean out blender, then add cashews, water, yeast, miso, chili powder, and garlic powder to blender.

Blend on high until smooth.

Slice baguette into four pieces, then halve these pieces.

Spread 1 tbsp corn and bean spread on four slices of the baguette.

Top with 2 tomato slices and vegan mozzarella.

On the other slices of bread, spread cashew "cheese"and close sandwiches.

Serve, or grill in a skillet over medium heat for 4 minutes per side to toast before serving.

Curry "Egg" Salad

A spicy and exotic take on tofu egg salad for those days when you need more flavor!

Serves: 4

Ingredients

1 diced stalk of celery
16oz drained firm tofu
1/3 cup vegan mayonnaise
1 chopped scallion
1 tsp curry powder
2 tsp prepared yellow mustard
3 tbsp nutritional yeast
1 tsp black salt (optional)
8 slices of thick bread
Toppings of your choice

Instructions

Slice tofu into six pieces and blot with paper towels.

Mash tofu in a bowl, then stir in celery and scallion.

In a separate bowl, combine mayonnaise with curry powder, mustard, and nutritional yeast.

Pour mixture over tofu and stir to mix flavors well.

Season with black salt, if desired.

Cover and chill for at least 2 hours.

Spread onto bread and top with your choice of toppings.

Serve.

Kale Sandwiches

This kale-based sandwich spread tastes great with any toppings you could want!

Serves: 4

Ingredients

2 rinsed kale leaves
15oz canned drained and rinsed chickpeas
1 peeled and diced carrot
1/3 cup vegan mayonnaise
2 tbsp nutritional yeast
1/4 cup parsley leaves
2 tsp yellow prepared mustard
2 sliced scallions
1/2 tsp curry powder
1 tbsp lemon juice
1/2 tsp ground cumin
1/2 tsp black pepper
Handful of fresh sprouts
Toppings of your choice
8 slices thick bread

Instructions

Place kale and carrot into a food processor or blender and pulse until chopped.

Add all ingredients except sprouts to blender and blend on high until mixed but still chunky.

Spread mixture onto sandwiches and top with sprouts and other toppings of your choice.

Serve.

Hummus Wrap

Grab an easy Mediterranean inspired hummus wrap for your lunch any day!

Serves: 1

Ingredients

- 1 wheat tortilla
- 1/4 sliced cucumber
- 1/4 sliced tomato
- 1/4 sliced avocado
- Handful baby greens
- 4 tbsp olive oil based hummus

Instructions

Spread tortilla with hummus.

Layer on baby greens.

Top with cucumbers and tomatoes.

Finish with avocado.

Roll up and enjoy.

Chapter 5 - Conclusion

Time for lunch, vegan style! Now that you have explored the pages of this book in full, you should be ready to prepare any of these simple and delicious vegan lunches. Just pick your favorite, gather the ingredients you need, and get ready to cook. The results will be amazing!

Two Awesome Free Gifts For You

I want to say "Thank You" for buying my book so I've put together a few, awesome free gifts for you.

The Essential Kitchen Series Cooking Hacks & Tips Book

&

100 Delicious New Recipes

These gifts are the perfect add-on to this book and I know you'll love them.

So visit link below to download you free gift now

www.GoodLivingPublishing.com/essential -kitchen